Daddy's Football Game © 2015 Len Mormino, Vission Enterprises LLC

All rights reserved. No part of this book may be reproduced or transmitted in any form or by any means, electronic or mechanical, including photocopying, recording, or by any information storage and retrieval system without written permission, except in the case of brief quotations embodied in critical articles and reviews.

Published by Vission Enterprises LLC
Middleton, Wisconsin
www.lenmormino.com

ISBN 978-0-692-54619-2

Library of Congress Number on file

To Mom and Pop....

for showing us how to

LOVE LOTS

WORK HARD

&

PLAY OFTEN

To Sus'....

for believing in my

IMAGINATION

Reflecting in the hall

on the bareness of new walls,

Mattie longs to decorate them

with the colors that make Fall.

She's still in her pajamas

craving pancakes with bananas

while her sisters and their mommy

pick up paint from Aunt Susanna.

She hears a click, the TV roars
with horns and crowds and cheers,

talking heads discussing teams,
commercials with root beer.

The clock begins to strike 12 tolls
as if it must proclaim,

"All quiet for the start of
Daddy's sacred football game!"

He doesn't listen very well
while that long show is on.

The house could be on fire for hours,
he still would not catch on.

But with Daddy all to herself
she knows that it's their chance,

to do some playing, painting, cooking,
dress up, and some dance!

The football is aflight and

Daddy's favorite player drops it.

Mattie settles in making good use of all her pockets.

And as she sets her dollhouse up across the tabletop,

Daddy screams out "Catch a ball!"

and all the neighbors stop.

A time out is called while

Mattie holds her daddy's cheeks,

kneeling there upon his lap and

glaring as she speaks.

"Daddy you did promise me

the next time we're alone,

you'd play house and anything I want

without a moan."

So......

Sliding down onto the floor, he grabs a daddy dolly.

Mattie takes it and instead gives him

the dog and mommy.

And while playing some hide and seek,

and tag and duck-duck-goosy,

they lose track of football

and who's winning or is losing.

Daddy barks "That's all, I'm done!"
and plops back on the couch,

folding up his grumpy arms
and scowling like a grouch.

Then just as he begins to grin
at his team's pass completion,

Mattie's tummy starts to growl
from sudden food depletion.

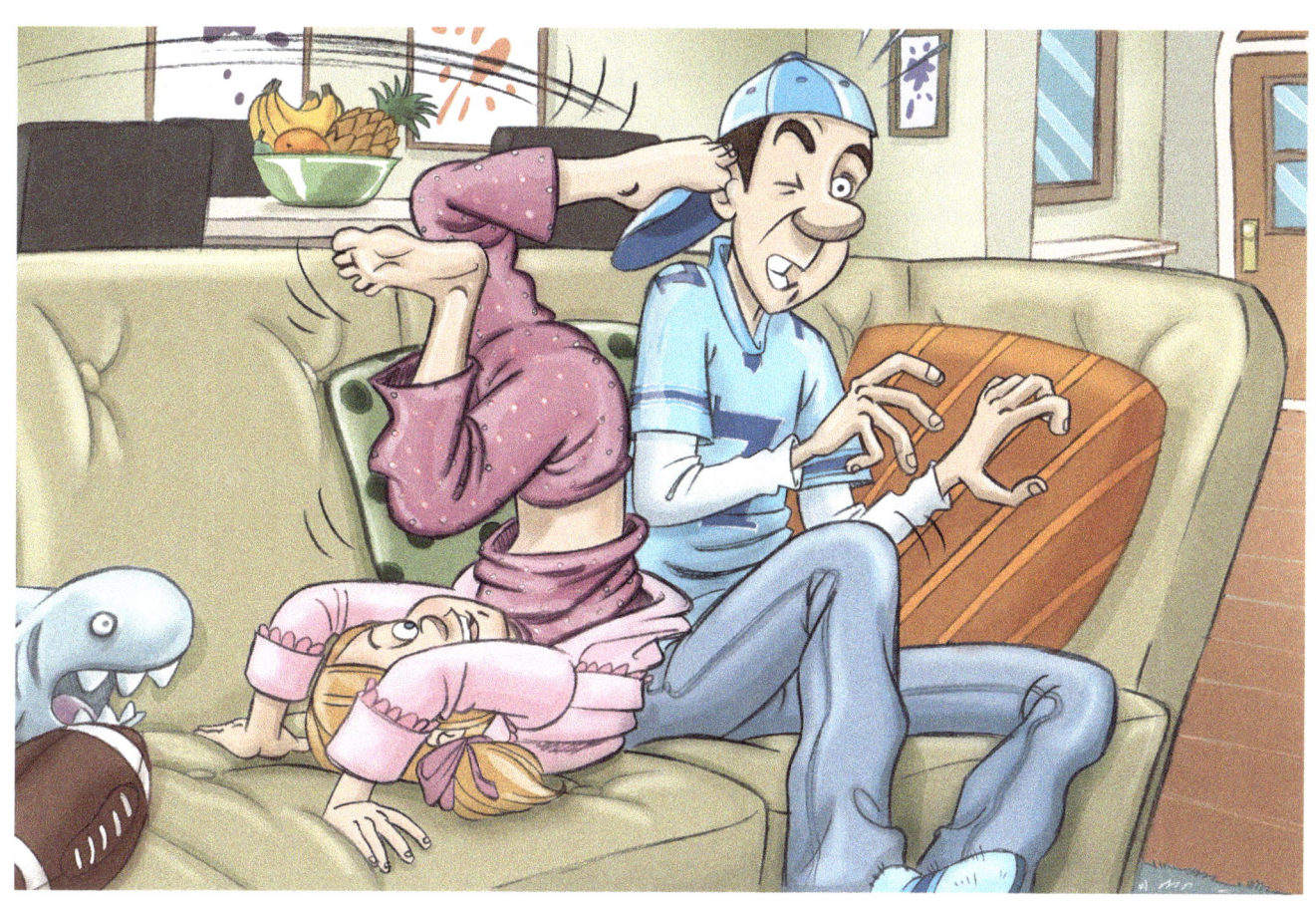

Next to him, upside down,

with her rump up in the air,

Mattie whines "I'm hungry"

as her big toe finds his ear.

So me-oh-my and with a sigh

he gives her the remote,

and in the kitchen Dad makes

hot dogs, beans, and root beer floats.

Mattie grabs some crackers, grapes,

a cheese called Dutch Hvarti,

fancy dishes, napkins,

and some tea cups; it's a party!

And finding a tiara with a

white dress that's perfection,

she slips them on her daddy

while he cries out "interception!"

While Dad begins to dine

and focus on the half time show,

Mattie sneaks below to paint

the nails on all his toes.

She teaches him to sip tea

with his nose up in the air,

hold his pinky arched

to make his bites more debonair.

They fingerpaint as penalties

make fans turn glum and groany.

They bake a wedding cake as

Mattie plans a ceremony.

And when the crowd goes wild because

those teams tied up the game,

Daddy says "I do" to

Mattie's Teddy Bear named Shane.

Neither seems to care much as

the ball begins to fumble.

They're busy setting dominos

across the floor to tumble.

Then messing up a field goal

also seems to go unnoticed,

while they dance the limbo to see

who can lean the lowest.

Suddenly a doorbell rings and

friends rush in the room,

quite enjoying Daddy Bride and

Shane his furry groom.

Mattie yells "Let's go play!" and

commands her troops outside,

leaving Daddy with Shane and his

team that came up dry.

But knocking on the window Mattie

yells through with a grin,

"Daddy, our team lost but boy

our playtime was a WIN!"

"In fact that game was fun and

that it's over's such a shame.

Will you come outside and

help US play a football game?"

THE END

"Daddy's Football Game"
is the second book in the "Mattie's World" series.
Want to see how Mattie took over her dad's favorite lunchtime meal?
Look for "Daddy's Macaroni" in Softcover Print (Amazon),
as an eBook (most e-Reader platforms),
and audio-eBook (iBooks) read by
the author and his daughters.

~~~~~~~~~~~~~~

About the Author and Illustrator

Len David Mormino has been a writer for music, lyrics, theater, children's books, counseling, and education since 1993. As a community and school counselor, he has enjoyed staying in touch with the hearts and language of youth and families. Growing up in the Chicago area in a fun-loving Jewish-Italian home, Len enjoyed all of the music, noise, food, and chaos that one can handle. He and his wife now live in a neighboring suburb of her hometown, Madison, Wisconsin. They like to get crazy with their 3 daughters and dog Marley. You can find more of Len's music and writing at www.lenmormino.com.

Nathalie Ortega has spent the last 15 years illustrating children's books with various techniques. Her works have been published internationally by many prestigious companies all around the world, including the USA, UK, Spain, Australia and many other countries. Publishers such as Pearson Education, Longman, Oxford University Press, and Harper Collins have her art in picture books, ELT, school books, and more. Nathalie loves her work, made at her home studio. She lives with her husband, son and two funny kitties, Chloé and Lilo. You can find more of her artwork at theillustratorsagency.com website.

www.ingramcontent.com/pod-product-compliance
Lightning Source LLC
Chambersburg PA
CBHW061818290426
44110CB00026B/2905